W9-BRV-948

# Take Two and Butter 'Em While They're Hot
## *by*
## Barbara Swell

Native Ground Music, Inc.

Order No. NGB-810     ISBN 1-883206-32-4

Copyright 1998 by Native Ground Music, Inc.
International Copyright Secured. All Rights Reserved

# HOT BREAD & FREE ADVICE

I f you want some hot bread and free advice, step into my grandmother's kitchen. Though she's been gone years, I can still see her puttering around her green enameled table, rolling out her famous sugar cookies. She's just been to the beauty shop and her silver hair is curled so nice. I can see her waving her rolling pin around above her ample bosom as she tells me "what's what" about life. Maybe she's giving me cooking advice, like *"Be sure the guests are sitting at the table before you take the biscuits out of the oven."* Then say, *"Take two and butter 'em while they're hot."* Or maybe it's pre-nuptial advice like *"Never let him see the string you lead him by."* and *"Tell him you love him every day."*

It was in the kitchen where I got to know the women in my family, making chicken pies with them side-by-side dusted with flour, in our starched cotton aprons. That's how I found out about my mother's childhood antics growing up in her small West Virginia town. Like the time her grandfather took her on a hike to the next town and she was to bring the picnic lunch, which she did. Bread crusts. Only bread crusts. Her grandfather was not pleased!

*My grandmother, Maude Smith*

Lessons of cooking, love, and wisdom continue to be learned in the kitchens of our family as the next generation sprouts wings and leaves home. My niece, Sara Webb begins an essay for a college application with, *"I come from a long line of strong women..."* And if you ask her how she came to know of these spicy women, she'll tell you it was over a bowl of warm blackberry cobbler with whipped cream in somebody's kitchen.

While this is a book of my family's favorite recipes, wisdom, and photos; you have family folklore waiting to be captured, too. You'll find some blank pages in the back of the book to record your own favorite family recipes and pearls of wisdom. Maybe something like, *"If you take the last biscuit on the plate, you have to kiss the cook."*

# TABLE OF CONTENTS

### Kitchen Wisdom
- *Get the candle lit before you blow out the match!*
- *Set a cracked plate down softly.*
- *When bugs give a party, they never ask the chickens.*
- *The dinner bell's always in tune for a hungry man.*
- *Never bet on 'taters before grabbin' time.*

# APPETIZERS

## CHEESE STRAWS

*My Aunt Mary of Athens, West Va. was a bridge party food expert.*
*Even if you're "bridge-impaired" like me, you'll still enjoy these.*

½ lb. sharp cheddar
    cheese grated
½ cup butter (1 stick)
1 cup self-rising flour
Pinch cayenne pepper
3 cups corn flakes

Whip cheese and butter until fluffy. Add cayenne and flour. If you don't have self-rising flour, substitute 1 cup all purpose flour mixed with ½ tsp. salt and 1 tsp. baking powder. Process until smooth. Measure 3 cups corn flakes, crush, then stir into cheese mixture. Form into small balls and flatten onto

*Martha and Johnnie Cole with their Granny Newman*

a greased cookie sheet. Bake at 350° for 10 minutes or until lightly browned.

## PESTO CHEESE BALL

8 oz. package of light cream cheese (not non-fat)
1 clove crushed garlic
A handful of fresh basil leaves
⅓ cup coarsely grated parmesan cheese
Chopped walnuts, pecans, or whole pine nuts

Blend cream cheese, garlic, and parmesan cheese in food processor until well mixed. Add fresh basil leaves and process until mixed in. Don't over-process or your cheeseball will be green! Form into a ball. Roll in nuts. Chill, then serve with crackers.

# Appetizers

## Aunt Mary's Pimento Cheese Spread

*I inherited Aunt Mary's Dormeyer mixer that she used when making her famous pimento cheese spread. She would put the cheese through the meat grinder attachment, then mix the other ingredients up in a bowl. Here is the recipe exactly as she gave it to me 25 years ago:*

> Pimento
> 1 lb. super sharp cheese
> Horseradish (she ground her own)
> Mustard
> Salt and pepper
> Salad dressing or mayonnaise

That's it. (I don't have her special touch, but best I can tell you is to grate the cheese, add a small jar of drained, chopped pimentos, then add rest of ingredients to taste and blend, then chill.) Serve with crackers.

### Friendship
*Brows may wrinkle, hair grow gray,*
*But friendship never knows decay.*

*A recipe that is old as time itself,*
*Yet always delightfully new.*
*They call it simply friendship,*
*Beloved, tried and true.*[4]

# Soups

## Steve's Brunswick Stew

*If you grew up in Brunswick County, Virginia, like my brother-in-law, Steve Webb did, you'd know that Brunswick Stew was originally created there in 1828 by camp cook, Uncle Jimmy Matthews, for a hunting party. Others have tried to claim this stew as their own, but in 1988, the Virginia General Assembly passed a resolution declaring Brunswick County, Va. as the original home of this famous stew. This heirloom recipe was passed on to Steve from his mother, Elsie Saunders Webb, a native of Brunswick County.*

1 very well cooked 3 lb. chicken with bones removed
4 whole potatoes      4 large diced onions
3 sliced carrots      1 quart tomatoes

Cook these ingredients in chicken broth until tender. Add enough water until it's the consistency you like, along with

1 box frozen lima beans, 1 large can corn
1 Tbs. sugar
lots of pepper, and a small piece of butter

Stir well and low simmer for about 30 minutes, or cook in a slow cooker for a few hours on low.

---

### Kitchen Wisdom

•*A robin's song is not pretty to a worm.*
•*Give me today's meat, yesterday's bread, last year's wine, and the doctor can go.*
•*An empty pot never boils.*
•*A watched pot never boils.*

# Soups

## Garden Fresh English Pea Soup

2 cups fresh or frozen peas
1 cup chicken broth
Pepper, fresh herbs

1 small onion, chopped
Whole milk

Cook the peas 5 minutes, until tender in a small amount of water. Saute onion in a little butter until translucent. Puree peas and onions with a steel blade in food processor or a blender. Add chicken broth and enough milk until it's the consistency you want. Heat, but DO NOT boil. Add pepper and whatever chopped fresh spices you have. Basil and thyme are good. Garnish with a dollup of sour cream.

*Southern Appalachian Photo Archive, Mars Hill College, N.C.*

### Character Traits, 1850's

- *She's as sassy as a parched pea.*
- *He's as ignorant of his virtue as a possum is a corncake.*
- *She's as good as a cranberry tart.*
- *She's as prim as a peapod.*[8]

# Soups

## Johnnie Otto's Soup Beans

*This recipe comes straight out of the Sugarlands in the Great Smoky Mountains of Tennessee where Mrs. Otto grew up. I got it via her back porch in Virginia. She's pictured below second from the left amongst half of her siblings.*

*Johnnie Cole Otto and her sisters*

"Cook some October beans until they're done with a hunk of salt pork about this big ($\frac{1}{3}$ of a fist). Don't use bacon...only thing bacon makes good is eggs! Add a potato and a chopped onion. Add water until it's the consistency you like. Cook until done. Serve it with fried cornbread."

## Fried Cornbread

"Make up a recipe of cornbread that's got enough flour in it to handle (omit egg). Put 4 pones (long patties) in each corner of a baking sheet and bake until done. Slice the pones long-ways and fry in a skillet with a little butter and oil."

---

### Mountain Wisdom
- *Learn from the mistakes of others, you won't have time to make them all yourself!*
- *Every pea helps fill the peck.*

---

*The Cole family next to their cabin in Tenn.*

# Soups

## Janet's Turkey Corn Chowder

*If you tell my sister, Janet, you're coming over for lunch on a cold and blustery day, you're likely to get a steaming bowl of this wonderful soup along with some fresh homemade bread.*

1 chopped onion sauted in ½ stick butter (or less)
2 cups chicken broth
3 cups diced cooked turkey or chicken
1 cup sliced celery
5 cubed potatoes
Cook until potatoes are tender then add:
      1 large can each corn kernals & creamed corn
      1 quart milk
Heat well, but don't boil. Before serving, sprinkle with parsley and paprika.

*Photo courtesy East Tenn. State University Photo Archives*

### Mountain Insults
• *He's slow as the seven year itch!*
• *She's so mean, she'd put a spider in your biscuit!*

# BREAD

## JOHNNIE OTTO'S BISCUITS

About 3 cups self-rising flour (*see note)
About ½ cup solid vegetable shortening
Whole milk

Johnnie Otto and sister, Martha Whaley

*"Mix the shortening in with the flour until crumbly. Add enough milk so you can handle the dough. Always use whole milk 'cause you could knock a bull down with a skim milk biscuit! Knead until it holds its shape good. Kneading doesn't hurt the dough like some folks say. Flour your board and roll it out until it's about an inch and a half thick. Cut straight down with a biscuit cutter dipped in flour. If you twist when cutting, the biscuits won't rise right. Cook in a hot oven until lightly browned. And remember...a good cook don't leave the kitchen! Have your guests sit at the table and when you pull the biscuits out of the oven say,* **Have a hot-en!"**

*Note: Mrs. Otto's favorite flour is called Virginia's Best Self Rising Flour from Big Spring Mill, Inc. of Elliston, Va. 24087. The mill's been operating since the mid-1800's and takes mail orders. They sell great cornmeal too!

---

### The Making of a Blue-Ribbon Cook

*"When I was a teen, Uncle Dick owned the Greystone Hotel on the Little Pigeon River in Gatlinburg, Tenn. One day, I was makin' biscuits for breakfast at the hotel, and I just kept a pan of 'em out and ran them over to the county fair at the Pi Phi school. I won second prize. They said they were browned just perfect, but needed a little more salt and they would've won first."* (And she's been winning blue ribbons ever since!) 　　　　　　　　　　-Johnnie Cole Otto

# BREAD

## MA BARKER'S DELICIOUS ROLLS

*"When I was growing up in Salem, W. Va, my dad owned Smith Brothers Grocery (pictured pg. 40-41). At age 16, I delivered groceries in our paneled truck, and I ate my way through the back door of all the good cooks in our small town. I always tried to deliver to Ma Barker between 4 and 6 p.m., hoping to have some of her delicious rolls as they came out of the oven."*

*-Nancy Smith Swell*

| | |
|---|---|
| 1 cup warm water | 1 cup room temp. milk |
| 3 cakes (2 pkg.) yeast | ½ cup sugar |
| 1½ tsp. salt | 6 Tbs. butter, melted |
| 1 or 2 eggs, well beaten | About 7 cups flour |

Dissolve yeast in water, then add salt, sugar, eggs, milk, and butter. Add enough flour to make a soft dough you can handle. Knead 15 minutes, then let rise until doubled in a buttered bowl covered with a towel. Make into rolls and let rise on a greased cookie sheet about 30 minutes. Bake in a pre-heated 350° oven until lightly browned. Is that my mother pulling into your driveway in an old paneled truck with a sack full of groceries?

## POUNDED BISCUITS

One quart flour
2 tsp. salt
½ tea cup soft butter
Milk

Mix salt and flour; work in butter and add enough milk to make a stiff dough. Knead a little, then whack with a rolling pin 15 minutes. Roll out, cut small, and tick with a fork. Put on greased cookie sheet and bake in a hot oven until lightly browned.

# BREAD

## CORNBREAD

1 cup stoneground cornmeal (white or yellow will do)
1 cup flour
3 tsp. baking powder
1 tsp. salt
2 or 3 Tbs. sugar
1¼ cup sweet milk
1 egg (optional)
½ stick butter, melted in an iron skillet in hot oven

Preheat oven to 400°. Mix dry and wet ingredients separately, then add wet to dry. Stir until blended. Pour into hot buttered skillet and bake until nicely browned.

*If the cornbread cracks while you're baking it, there will be an increase in the family.*[9]

*My father, Leon Swell (pictured 4th from left)), with his family and friends*

# BREAD

## CHALLAH

*My paternal grandparents emigrated to the U.S. from Russia and Poland in the early 1920's. Grandpa made his living peddling dry goods in the Bronx section of New York City during a time when the town was made up of separate neighborhoods whose residents kept the language and customs of their native lands. I remember his English was broken, yet he spoke fluent Russian, Italian, Polish, and Yiddish. They kept a kosher kitchen and my Grandmother, Bessie, would serve Challah on Fridays for Shabbat. These braided loaves are beautiful.*

| | |
|---|---|
| 2 cups warm whole milk | 2 tsp. salt |
| 2 Tbs. honey | 4 Tbs. melted butter |
| 1 pkg. dried yeast | 1 or 2 eggs, beaten |
| Unbleached bread flour | |

Dissolve yeast in warm milk and add honey. Let it sit for 10 minutes then add salt, butter, and eggs. Add enough flour until you have a soft dough. Turn out on a floured board and knead 15 minutes until elastic. Put in a buttered bowl to rise until doubled. Punch down and divide in half. Divide each half into three sections which you roll out into long "snakes". Braid the loaf, tucking ends under at top and bottom. Place both loaves on a buttered cookie sheet to rise until doubled. You can brush uncooked loaves with a little beaten egg and sprinkle sesame seeds on top if you like. Bake in a pre-heated 375° oven until browned (25-40 minutes).

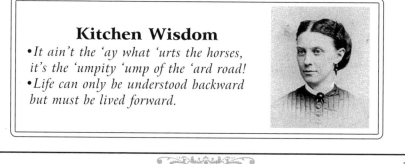

### Kitchen Wisdom
• *It ain't the 'ay what 'urts the horses, it's the 'umpity 'ump of the 'ard road!*
• *Life can only be understood backward but must be lived forward.*

# BREAD

### RUSTIC BREAD

**Sponge:**
²/₃ cup warm milk          4 Tbs. sugar
¹/₃ cup water              1 cup white all-purpose flour
1 pkg. dry yeast (about 1 Tbs.)

Combine these ingredients and let stand until bubbly, about 2 hours. Then add:

1 pkg. dry yeast dissolved in 2 cups room temp. water
3 tsp. salt
Bread flour

Add enough flour to batter to make a dough you can handle. Knead until elastic. I beat this dough with a rolling pin instead of kneading by hand. Let rise in a large buttered bowl until doubled. It won't take long because you made a sponge. Punch dough down and divide into 3 portions. Form each loaf into a shape you like (torpedo shapes fit well into the oven). Dredge top in flour and lay to rise on breadboard sprinkled with cornmeal. Cover with a towel until doubled. After about 30 minutes, pre-heat oven to 400°. If you have a bread stone, put it on the bottom rack.

When bread is almost doubled, make shallow slashes on top with a sharp knife or razor blade. Carefully place bread on baking stone (or on greased baking sheet) in hot oven. Put a shallow pan of hot water on top rack of oven and quickly close the door. Bake for 15 minutes then turn heat down to 350° and bake 15 more minutes. Remove pan of water and bake until top is nicely browned.
***Whole Wheat bread:** Substitute ½ of flour with stone-ground wheat, and add ½ cup honey instead of sugar.

> • *There's not a pot so crooked that there isn't a lid to fit it.*
> • *A person who gets all wrapped up in herself makes a mighty small package.*

# BREAD

## TORTA

Make Rustic Bread recipe, dividing the dough into three balls. For each Torta, take two thirds of one ball and roll it into a large circle. If it won't roll, let it rest 5 minutes. Place the circle in a buttered casserole dish so that the sides hang over the edges of the pan. Top the dough with:

- •A layer of white cheese (Swiss or a smoked variety)
- •A layer of thinly sliced Italian plum tomatoes
- •Fresh or dried basil, a pinch of fresh, chopped garlic, and optional ingredients-thinly sliced purple onion, ham, green pepper, black olives.

Top the last layer with thinly sliced cheese. Roll the last portion of dough into a circle and place on top of casserole. Overlap the edges of dough from the bottom over the top dough. Slice steam holes in the top and bake at 350° about 30-40 minutes until browned.

*A smile is a light in the window of your face to show your heart is at home.*[4]

Scruggs, the miller"     Photo by Margaret Morely, N.C. Dept. Archives and History

15

# HOLIDAY BREAD

## SCANDANAVIAN SWEET BREAD

*We give these beautiful moist loaves of bread for winter holiday gifts. This recipe makes 3 loaves.*

| | |
|---|---|
| 2 cups warm whole milk | 2 packages dry yeast |
| ½ cup sugar | ½ cup warm water |
| 1 tsp. salt | 2 Tbs. sugar |
| 1 tsp. ground cardamom | 1 or 2 eggs |
| ½ cup melted butter | White flour |

Mix milk, sugar, salt, cardamom, butter, and egg. In a separate bowl, dissolve yeast and 2 Tbs. sugar in ½ cup warm water. Combine all and add enough flour to make a soft dough. Knead until elastic about 10-15 minutes. Let rise in a greased bowl until doubled. Punch down and divide dough into thirds, then divide each third into three portions. Roll out into long strands and braid each of the three loaves of bread. Place on buttered baking sheets and allow to double again. Bake in a pre-heated 350° oven until lightly browned. When bread has almost cooled, drizzle with glaze.

**Glaze:** Combine 4 Tbs. soft butter with ½ box powdered sugar. Add juice and rind of 1 lemon. Adjust sugar and juice until you have a glaze that is pourable but not runny.

Luella and Frederick Miller fishing on Lake Hopatcong

# HOLIDAY BREAD

## HOLIDAY SAFFRON BREAD 1895

*My friend, Pam Budd, shared this recipe with me. It comes from her great grandmother, Luella Miller. After her 3 daughters had grown, Luella would get up real early, cook lunch and dinner, then head off to lake Hopatcong in her little boat to fish the day out (see photo left). If it was winter, why she'd ice-fish. When Luella wasn't fishing, cooking, or vegetable gardening, she worked at home for a business which crocheted around the edges of women's undershirts in the pre-lingerie days. When I asked Pam what she remembered about this Holiday Saffron Bread, she said, THE SMELL!!! When her mother or grandmother would make it, the whole neighborhood could smell the sweet fragrance of the saffron.*

| | |
|---|---|
| ½ cup potato water | 2 pkg. dried yeast |
| 2 cups scalded milk | 2 to 4 eggs |
| 1 cup butter | 2 tsp. salt |
| ½ cup saffron tea | 1 box raisins |
| 1 cup mashed potatoes | flour (10-12 cups) |
| 1 cup sugar | |

Mix sugar, butter, eggs, and salt until smooth. Make saffron tea with 1 Tbs. crumbled saffron stirred into ½ cup water. Stir in lukewarm liquids, potatoes, yeast and mix well. Add enough flour to make a soft dough. Knead 10-15 minutes until elastic. Mix in raisins after kneading, then let rise in a buttered bowl until doubled. Punch dough down, place in buttered loaf pans and let rise again until doubled. Bake in a preheated 350° oven until browned 30-40 minutes.

*__Note:__ Saffron is hard to find and expensive, but the taste is unique. Often, you can find little glass tubes of a few strands in speciality stores...and a few strands is better than none. If you can't find saffron, the bread is still good without it. Just be sure to keep liquid amounts the same.*

---

### Wise Sayin's

• *Short visits make long friends.*
• *More cotton will grow on a crooked row than a straight one.*[1]

# Holiday Bread

## Stollen

*Slice this rich holiday bread thinly and toast. It will keep well wrapped in plastic for about 2 weeks. It takes a little practice to get this special bread right, but when you do, people will be clamoring for it...and you can add your name to it!*

**Soak:** 2 cups chopped dried fruit in ½ cup warm rum to plump. A combination of dried cherries, pineapple, apricots, and raisins is tasty.

**Sponge:** Stir 1 pkg. dried yeast and 1 cup sugar into 1 cup warm milk until dissolved. Add one cup flour. Let sponge "work" for about an hour until bubbly.

**Dough:** Combine 1 cup warm milk, 1 pkg. dry yeast, 2 tsp. salt (1 tsp. less if butter is salted), 1 egg, 1 stick butter, zest of a lemon. Add the sponge, the drained fruit, and blend well. Add enough unbleached all-purpose flour so that the dough clears the sides of the bowl. Knead until dough is springy, about 5-10 minutes. Add as little flour as possible to your bread board. Put dough in a greased bowl to rise about 1½ hours.

Divide dough into 2 or 3 portions. Flatten each portion into an oval (1 inch thick), brush tops with melted butter and sprinkle with cinnamon sugar. Fold the ovals in half "long ways" with the top half just about 1 inch shy of the bottom half. Let rise on a lightly floured surface about 1 hour covered with a damp towel. Place loaves on a buttered cookie sheet and bake about 30 minutes in 350° preheated oven. Cover with foil if they're getting too brown. When bread is cool, rub well with powdered sugar.

# MEAT DISHES

*Great Smoky Mt. National Park*

*"Strings of fish"*

## DELL'S ITALIAN SPAGHETTI

*Dell owned the City Diner in Salem, W.Va. where my mom grew up. You just had to have a plate of his spaghetti after church on Sunday. He was also famous for his salad dressing...and you could buy a mason jar of it to go, too.*

| | |
|---|---|
| 3 cans tomato paste | Salt and pepper |
| 1 chopped onion | 1 Tbs. sugar |
| 2 cloves chopped garlic | Ground cloves to taste |
| 1 #2 can tomatoes | 2 quarts tomato juice |
| 1 lb. ground pork | Dash chili powder |

Cook pork and drain off fat. Add onions, garlic and saute until translucent. Add other ingredients and cook 4-6 hours.

**Meat Balls:** Combine 1 lb. ground pork, ½ cup grated cheese, 3 slices crumbled bread, 2 tsp. chopped parsley, and 2 eggs. Cook in a little olive oil until done.

Serve sauce on hot spaghetti noodles and top with meat balls. Omit meat for a marinara sauce if desired.

# MEAT

Y ou'd be hard-pressed to find Ground Meat Whirls or Ham Croquettes on the tables of many folks these days. But in times past, foods like these were a dead give-away that you'd entered the home of a good cook who knew how to use up leftovers creatively and was thrifty to boot!

## GROUND MEAT WHIRLS

1 lb. ground meat
Pinch salt
2 Tbs. chopped green pepper
2 Tbs. flour
½ cup chopped onion
½ cup water
⅓ cup chopped celery
Pepper to taste
1 recipe biscuit dough

Cook meat, drain off fat. Add vegetables and cook until tender. Combine flour and water and add enough to other ingredients to thicken. Roll out biscuit dough jelly-roll fashion, spread meat mixture evenly over it, roll up and slice off one inch thick. Bake on greased cookie sheet at 400° until brown.

*So. Appalachian Photo Archive, Mars Hill College*

## HAM CROQUETTES

2 cups ground cooked ham
1 Tbs. chopped parsley
1 cup mashed potatoes
1 Tbs. chopped onion

1 Tbs. water
1 egg, beaten
Dried bread crumbs

Mix ham, parsley, potatoes, and onion. Form into patties. Dip patties into the beaten egg mixed with water, then dip in bread crumbs. Saute in a little butter in a skillet or bake in the oven at 400° until both sides are browned.

# MEAT

## CHILI CORN PONE PIE

You can make a vegetarian version of this pie by omitting meat and adding another can of kidney beans.

Chili:
1 lb. ground beef, browned
1 chopped onion
2 tsp. chili powder

2 cans tomatoes
2 cans kidney beans
Dash red wine

Cook above ingredients until it looks done. Adjust the liquid with water to reach the consistency you like. Pour hot chili into an oblong, glass baking dish. Top with ½ recipe of cornbread batter. You may want to add a little extra milk to the batter to make it pour easier. Bake at 400° until cornbread's done (about 20-25 minutes). Throw some cheddar cheese on top when you serve it.

*"The end of a day's work." Great Smoky Mt. National Park*

### Food Insults, 1856
- *You're straight as a beanpole stuck up on end!*
- *Your mouth's puckered up like you been eatin' unripe persimmons!*
- *You got less brains than an oyster!*
- *You're as mean as dog pie!*
- *Your face looks like you been fed on crab apples for a "hull" month!*
- *You don't know beans when the bag's open![8]*

# MEAT

## CHICKEN PIE

*I used to watch my grandmother toss this together effortlessly. She had about 12 inches of counter space to work with and she'd be covered with flour when she was finished.*

Boil a 3 lb. chicken until done, de-bone and cook the broth down to 2 cups. Cook up some vegetables (green beans, peas, carrots, corn...whatever you have) along with 2 white potatoes. Combine vegetables, chicken, 2 chopped hard-boiled eggs, the broth, and 3 Tbs. flour dissolved in a little cold water. Place in a baking dish and top with biscuits or a vented pastry crust. Bake at 400° about 20-25 minutes until bubbly and browned. Put it on the table after everyone's seated.

## MOCK CHICKEN SALAD

*In case you have pigs and don't want to eat your chickens. Recipes such as this were abundant in times when certain food items were scarce.*

2 cups roast pork, cut in cubes
1 cup chopped celery
4 chopped olives
Red pepper
Mayonnaise
Mix well and serve chilled.

### Kitchen Wisdom
- *Talk is cheap, but it takes money to buy whiskey.*
- *There are more ways to kill a dog than by choking him to death on hot butter.*
- *Lick by lick, the cow ate the grindstone.*
- *If you make your bed hard, you can turn over more often.*[1]

# Meat

## Orange Chicken

Brown a cut up chicken in a little hot oil. Place it in a shallow baking dish and pour over it:

1 cup orange juice

1 cup dry white wine

½ cup raisins

½ cup sliced almonds

1 Tbs. sugar

½ tsp. grated fresh ginger

Salt & pepper to taste

Bake at 350° for 45 minutes until much of liquid is cooked down and chicken is done. Baste as you bake.

## Tipsy Pork Chops

Marinate pork chops in a mixture of:

    Bourbon

    Chopped garlic

    Brown sugar

    Fresh grated ginger

Grill or bake in oven until done.

## Bonnie's Chicken

*My sister-in-law, Bonnie Neustein, is famous for this chicken that she cooks for hours in a slow oven. She used to make huge pans of it for her boys while they were growing up.*

Lay chicken pieces (any are fine, thighs and legs are best) in a foil-lined baking dish. Pour this mixture over:

1 cup brown sugar

1 cup soy sauce

¾ cup sherry or white wine

1 Tbs. dry mustard

Chopped garlic

Grated fresh ginger

Bake at 300° for about 2 hours until liquid is absorbed. Baste and turn chicken over as needed.

# MEAT

## SALMON LOAF

1 large can salmon
1 small minced onion
1 egg
½ tsp. celery seed
½ cup milk
Pepper to taste
8 Saltine crackers
Bacon

Mix above ingredients well. Place two slices of bacon on the bottom of a buttered loaf pan. Form mixture into a loaf shape and put in pan. Top with two more slices of bacon and bake in a 350° oven about 45 minutes. If you want to get fancy, you can shape the mixture so it looks like a fish and poke in half an olive for an eyeball, then bake in a buttered oblong glass dish.

## CRAB CAKES

1 cup crab meat
1 egg, beaten
½ onion, minced
Chopped parsley
½ green or red pepper
Bread crumbs
Black pepper

Combine crab, onion, pepper, egg, and parsley. Add just enough bread crumbs to bind. Form into patties and saute until browned in a little butter. Serve with lemon wedges and either cocktail or tartar sauce.

# VEGETABLES

Just about everybody who raises a kitchen garden has a stubborn preference for certain vegetable varieties. I made my first garden in 1976 after Grandmother sat me down at her kitchen table and told me what catalogs to get which seeds out of. Here's her seed list:

| | |
|---|---|
| Sweet corn | *Silver Queen* |
| Bush bean | *White Half-runner* |
| Lima bean | *Fordhook* |
| Carrot | *Royal Chantenay* |
| Beet | *Little Ball* |
| Yellow squash | *Seneca Butterbar* |
| Zucchini | *Aristocrat* |
| Lettuce | *Buttercrunch* |
| Tomato | *Better Boy* |
| | *Beefsteak* |

*Great Smoky Mt. National Park*

*"Sarah Parton and her shuck beans"*

---

## Vegetable Superstitions

- *Put bean strings on the path to the spring for a good crop next year.*
- *You will raise one hundred bushels of corn for each white stalk you find in your field.*
- *If you eat corn out of a tomato bowl, you will eat corn cake out of a musk melon the following year.*
- *If a farmer has the brim of his hat turned up in front, he has corn for sale.*
- *If one eats a buck-eye, his head will turn around.*
- *You will have bad luck if you eat celery.*
- *Eat a pickle to settle your love.*

# VEGETABLES

## SCALLOPED POTATOES

5 large potatoes, sliced thin
1²/₃ cup milk
Pinch salt
Grated cheese

1 onion chopped
1 Tbs. butter
3 Tbs. flour

Boil potatoes 5 minutes and drain. Place in a buttered casserole dish. Saute onion in butter. Dissolve flour in a little cold milk and add along with remaining milk to onions. Heat and pour over potatoes. Cover with foil and bake at 350° until potatoes are almost tender. Top with cheese.

## LAURA'S PARMESAN POTATOES

*When my little sister, Laura, was about 8 yrs. old, we called her "Laura-Potato-Chip-Swell" because she knew what to do to a bag of chips. She still has a flair for the potato.*

½ large potato per person (slice ¼ in. thick length-wise)
2 Tbs. butter
1 tsp. basil
½ tsp. paprika
Pinch garlic powder and pepper
Grated parmesan cheese

Melt butter and add other ingredients. Brush potatoes on both sides with mixture and place on a cookie sheet. Broil 8-9 minutes until brown. Turn, sprinkle with cheese and broil until brown.

# VEGETABLES

I found my all-time favorite cookbook among my Aunt Mary's time-worn, treasured recipe books after she died. It's called "Oppis Guet's Vo Helvetia." Eleanor Mailloux of Helvetia, W.Va. wrote this book of recipes, cures, and household hints, to commemorate the town's centennial in 1969. She shares recipes, stories, and folk wisdom passed down from the Swiss families that settled into this area in such a way that you feel like you're sitting at her kitchen table. My grandfather used to travel to Helvetia to buy home-made Swiss cheese to sell in his grocery.

## ROSTI

*A Swiss potato pizza.*
Boil one large unpeeled potato per person until done. Chill at least 8 hours. Peel skins off and grate potato. Melt some butter in an iron skillet and put peeled potatoes in so that you have a large pancake. Flatten slightly so that potatoes stick together. Cook on medium low heat until browned on the bottom. This part is a bit tricky...to turn, grab a plate and flip the Rosti onto it uncooked side down. Melt some more butter in the bottom of the skillet and slide the Rosti onto it. Don't worry if it falls apart. Cook until underside is browned, then top like you would a pizza with any of these toppings:

> **Wild or tame cooked mushrooms**
> **Sliced black olives**
> **Green pepper and onions**
> **Cooked ham or sausage (not pepperoni)**
> **Pineapple slices (this is our favorite)**

Sprinkle topping(s) with grated white cheese like Swiss, Havarti, or Muenster, and broil until bubbly. Serve out of the hot skillet and don't forget the fresh ground pepper!

---

*The board is bare that does not share the laughter in the lamplight.*
*-Eleanor Mailloux*

---

# Vegetables

## Sweet-Potato Casserole

Sweet Potatoes (1 medium per person)
Brown Sugar                         1 egg
Chopped walnuts or pecans           Cinnamon

Peel and boil sweet potatoes until done. Mash, and add brown sugar to taste, 1 beaten egg (regardless of number of potatoes), and as many nuts as you like. Throw in a pinch of cinnamon, then put mixture in a buttered casserole dish. Bake at 350° about 30 minutes. You can put marshmallows on top and brown...especially for Thanksgiving.

## Cucumber Salad

*Here's a summer staple for cucumber season. Crunchy, fresh picked pickling cukes are great. I like to use the long-skinny-dark-spiny skinned Japanese varieties unpeeled.*

Cucumbers, peeled and sliced thin
Onions, sliced thin
Rice or white wine vinegar
Sugar
Fresh chopped herbs of your choice

Place cucumbers and onions in a bowl. Cover with a mixture of $^2/_3$ vinegar to $^1/_3$ water, and add sugar to taste. Let this chill at least 2 hours and serve with fresh herbs sprinkled on top.

### Good Luck Rhymes
*One for sorrow, two for joy,*
*Three for a letter, four for a boy,*
*Five for silver, six for gold,*
*Seven for a secret that's never been told.*

*A whistling gal and a flock of sheep*
*Are two good things for a farmer to keep.*

# VEGETABLES

**B**ack when we were kids, my two sisters and I would ride the train each summer to visit my grandmother in W. Va. and it seems her big garden was always in full swing. She'd sit us on the front porch glider with a lap full of newspapers that she'd pile high with fresh picked half-runner beans...and set us to work stringin'. We didn't mind because we knew exactly what we'd be eating that night for dinner. Her summer beans, monstrous just-picked Beefsteak tomatoes, Silver Queen corn on the cob, hot biscuits and a smoked pork chop. Maybe a peach cobbler for dessert. You could visit any one of us now some hot August evening, and my sisters and I would be serving up that very same meal. Dinner's at 6 o'clock. Don't be late!

## SUMMER STRING BEANS

*I say string beans, because bean variety is very important here. Beans with strings have the most flavor, I don't care what the seed catalogs say. Choose half-runners or pole beans for the best flavor. Those crispy, little beans won't hold up to long cooking times.*

String and snap as many beans as you like. Brown a couple pieces of bacon, ham or lean salt pork in a sauce pan (remove most of the fat) and add beans, then cover with water. Cook the beans about 30-45 minutes. Be sure that they don't run out of water, but that juices are cooked down. Now here's the important part. After you put the beans on your plate, top with a mixture of cut up home-grown tomatoes and diced onions.

# VEGETABLES

Home-made hominy is nothing like the kind you buy in a can. It's in a class by itself, but it does take some time to prepare. Martha Cole Whaley grew up in what's now the Great Smoky Mt. National Park in Tennessee. She's been making hominy since she was a child living in a cabin with her parents and 12 siblings. Martha still makes her home in Gatlinburg, Tennessee, where she lives a modern life....except for her cooking and hominy making.

## MARTHA WHALEY'S HOME-MADE HOMINY

You'll need about 1 quart of dry Hickory King white field corn for this. It's hard to find, but seed catalogs that sell heirloom "dent" field corns will suggest varieties that are good for hominy or cornmeal. Next, you'll need 1 lb. hard-wood ashes. Martha says, "Oak is awfully good." Make or find a muslin sack to put the ashes in. Cover corn with water in an enamel pan, throw in the tied-off muslin bag of ashes and cook a couple hours. When you can pick up a kernel and the skin slips off, start the rinsing process. Pour the water out and rinse the corn several times in cold water. Cover corn with fresh water and cook 30 minutes, then rinse well. Repeat the rinse-cook-rinse process 2 or 3 more times until the cooking water is completely clear. (The ashes are producing lye, so it's very important to rinse-cook-rinse repeatedly to be sure all the lye's out).

To serve, saute the hominy in butter, add salt to taste and lots of fresh ground pepper.

### Kitchen Wisdom 1844
- *An ounce of experience is worth a pound of theory.*
- *A broken egg can never be mended.*
- *Never give up as long as there's a pea in the gourd.*[8]

# VEGETABLES

## PESTO

*Pesto is best made using the "eyeball" method. Experiment with different amounts of ingredients and different varieties of basil, or try oregano, thyme, or cilantro.*

Fresh basil (washed and dried)
Parsley (washed and dried)
Grated parmesan cheese
Extra virgin olive oil
Minced fresh garlic
Pine nuts or walnuts

Fill food processor with ½ basil and ½ parsley. Add about ½ cup cheese, 1 or 2 cloves garlic, and a small handful of nuts. Process until chopped and drizzle in olive oil. I use very little oil...add what you like. Grind until it's as finely chopped as you can get it. Serve immediately on top of hot pasta. If you make it ahead of time, put it in a bowl and cover with a thin layer of olive oil to keep it from turning brown. Keeps well in refrigerator or you can freeze it.

## PESTO SQUASH

Slice yellow squash in rounds ¼ inch thick. Put on a buttered cookie sheet and broil in the middle of the oven until very lightly browned. Flip the squash and heat 2 or 3 minutes. Take out of the oven and cover each piece with a little pesto, then top with a few shreds of mozzarella or parmesan cheese. Broil until bubbly and serve immediately.

# Vegetables

## Summer Squash Casserole

Yellow or zucchini squash, sliced into very thin rounds
Onion, sliced
Tomato, sliced thin

Cornbread stuffing
Yellow cheese, grated

Butter a casserole dish and layer squash, onions, and tomatoes. Top with cheese, then buttered stuffing or bread crumbs, and cover tightly with foil. Bake at 350° for about 30 minutes. Uncover and bake until breadcrumbs are browned.

*"John Gregory, almost 7' tall"    Great Smoky Mt. National Park*

## Fried Green Tomatoes

Select tomatoes that are just about to start changing color....not little hard immature ones. Slice about ¼ inch thick. Cover with a mixture of cornmeal, salt, and pepper. Fry in a small amount of butter or oil (or a combination of both) on low heat until browned on both sides and tender in the middle. You can fry yellow or zucchini squash the same way.

### When to Cut Your Fingernails

*Cut your fingernails on Monday, cut them for news.*
*Cut them on Tuesday, get a new pair of shoes.*
*Cut them on Wednesday, you cut them for wealth.*
*Cut them on Thursday, you cut them for health.*
*Cut them on Friday, you cut them for sorrow;*
*Cut them on Saturday, see your sweetheart tomorrow;*
*Cut them on Sunday, it's safety you seek;*
*But the devil will have you the rest of the week.[5]*

# VEGETABLES

## FRESH TOMATO SALAD

*It's worth the wait to make this during tomato season. Use just-picked full-flavored big tomatoes. You can find fresh mozzarella in cheese shops if you don't live near an Italian grocery.*

Slice tomatoes ¼ inch thick. Arrange on a platter slices of tomato alternated with fresh mozzarella cheese. Sprinkle with shreds of fresh basil and drizzle Balsamic vinegar or Italian dressing on top. Sprinkle with fresh-ground pepper and throw on a few brine-ripened black olives.

*"An apple paring bee"*  *Photo by Margaret Morley,*  *N.C. Dept. Archives & History*

# CONDIMENTS

**D**uring the depression and before, many food items were scarce and you had to "make-do" with what you could get your hands on. Savory sauces and relishes

*Aunt Lula Smith Wilcox*

were depended on to add zip to the meal. You can make relish from anything you have an abundance of growing in your garden. Next winter, open up a pint of summer canned chili sauce or picalilli and you and your meal will perk up!

The first four recipes came straight out of the now tattered and yellowed cookbook my W. Va. grandmother put together for herself early in her marriage to my grandfather. He was also a good cook.

## AUNT LULA'S PEPPER RELISH

*Lula was my great Aunt. This is exactly how the recipe was entered in Grandmother's cookbook:*

| | |
|---|---|
| 4 heads cabbage | 3 small onions |
| 15 green peppers | 5¢ worth mustard seed |
| 5 red bell peppers | 5¢ worth celery seed |

¾ cup sugar heated with 1 quart vinegar. Cool and pour over cabbage and peppers.

**\*Author's note:** Shred the cabbage. Finely chop peppers and onions and place mixture in sterile pint jars. Sprinkle a little mustard and celery seed in each jar, then fill jars with hot sugar/vinegar mixture. Follow directions for hot water bath canning in an all purpose cookbook. If you want to make relish in smaller quantities for your use now, let sugar/vinegar mixture cool before adding to vegetables and keep relish in glass jars in the refrigerator. Give some to your neighbor, too!

## CHILI SAUCE

2 dozen tomatoes
3 green peppers
3 red peppers
3 onions

½ cup sugar
2 tsp. salt
1 tsp. cinnamon
1 quart vinegar

**\*Directions:** Peel tomatoes by dipping briefly in boiling water then chop. Chop peppers and onions finely then add them to the tomatoes along with other ingredients. Simmer at least an hour until thick. Pour into about 10 sterilized pint jars and seal.

*"Food safe" Great Smoky Mt. National Park*

## PICCALILLI

½ gallon ripe tomatoes
½ gallon green tomatoes
½ cup salt
6 green peppers
3 sweet red peppers
6 small onions

3½ cup sugar
½ tsp. mustard seed
½ tsp. whole cloves
2 tsp. celery seed
¼ tsp. allspice
3½ cup vinegar

Chop tomato fine, add salt, and let stand several hours. Drain thoroughly. Chop peppers and onions fine and add to tomatoes. Combine spices and tie up in a muslin bag. Boil vinegar, sugar and spices about 3 minutes and add vegetables, simmering for 45 minutes. Skim off foam. Pack into sterilized jars.

---

### Insults
• *He's not as big as a pound of soap after a hard day's washing.*
• *She's not worth a June bug with a cat bird after her.*

---

# CONDIMENTS

## SPICED PEACH PICKLE, 1915

*"Peel peaches (dip in boiling water 10 seconds) and stick one or two cloves in each one. Make syrup of 1 qt. vinegar and 1 cup sugar. Put in some whole spices or, if ground, tie up in a muslin bag. When syrup is boiling, put in the peaches but be sure the syrup covers them. Let boil long enough for peaches to become tender but firm, drop them one by one into jars and cover with hot syrup. Water bath process and keep 'em till Christmas or Thanksgiving, or the Fourth o' July or Sunday or something."*

## HOW TO TELL IF COMPANY'S COMING

- Take two pieces of bread at one time, hungry company's coming.
- Drop a knife, a man's coming; a fork, a woman.
- If your nose itches, company's coming.
- Drop a dishrag, someone nastier than you is coming.
- Leave a kettle uncovered, company's coming.
- If a straw falls from a broom that's being used, company's coming.[1]
- If a lightning bug gets into your house at night, a stranger's coming.
- A rooster crowing at your back door means a caller.
- When a spider builds a web in your house, expect a caller the same color as the spider.
- If you drop a wet dish cloth and it falls loose, a woman's coming. If it falls in a knot, a man is coming.[5]

# DESSERTS

A unt Ada was a strong-minded fiesty woman who died a few years back...just short of her 100th birthday. I remember long-ago lazy summer days spent leaning on her pea trellis chomping peas right off the vine. With a twinkle in her eye, she'd act like we kids were a bother, then she'd bring out a plate of these crunchy cookies for us that would be gone as soon as they hit the table.

## AUNT ADA'S OATMEAL COOKIES

1 cup brown sugar
1 cup white sugar
1 cup butter
2 eggs
1 tsp. vanilla

¾ cup flour
1 tsp. soda
1 tsp. salt
½ cup chopped walnuts
3 cups oats (not quick)

Cream butter and sugar, add eggs and vanilla. Add dry ingredients, then stir in nuts and oats. Grease a cookie sheet and place small spoonfuls far apart as these cookies need room to spread out. Bake at 350° 10-15 minutes until browned. While warm (but not hot), remove cookies to cool on wire cookie racks. If they stick to pan, just warm them up a bit to remove them. You'll need to wash and regrease your pan after each batch for best results. Keep in a tin or they will lose their crunch.

*Aunt Ada Smith Sommerville*

*But in the mud and scum of things*
*There always, always, something sings.*
*                              -Ralph Waldo Emerson*
*Looks like everything in the world comes right if we jes'*
*wait long enough.                    -Mrs. Wiggs*

# DESSERTS

The much anticipated tin of Lebkuchen arrives in the mail like clockwork every year right before Christmas. I wish the postman would make a mistake and deliver it to us, but it heads to its rightful owners...our neighbors Jean and Chris. Chris' grandmother, Helen Grass, sent these out every year to her friends and relatives from her citrus farm in California until she died a few years ago. Since then, her daughter, Bobbie Rogers, has carried on the tradition. Don't be scared off by the lengthy instructions. They're delicious and fat-free, too!

## GRAMMIE GRASS' LEBKUCHEN

| | |
|---|---|
| 1 cup honey | 5 cups flour |
| 1 cup molasses | 1 tsp. salt |
| 2 small lemons and rind | 1 tsp. baking soda |
| 2 eggs, beaten | 2 tsp. cinnamon |
| ½ cup brown sugar | 2 tsp. ginger |
| 2 cups walnuts | 2 tsp. nutmeg |
| 1 lb. citron | 2 tsp. mace |
| 1 tsp. vanilla | 1 tsp. almond extract |

Bring honey and molasses to boil and cool. Add lemon juice and rind, and beaten eggs . Stir in brown sugar, vanilla, and almond extract. Put citron and walnuts through a grinder and add to mixture. (You can grind in food processor.) Sift together dry ingredients and add to first mixture. Batter will be very thick. Cover with a plate and refrigerate overnight to let the flavors blend. Next day, grease right to edges of two 15 x 10 inch cookie sheets. Divide batter in half, and with a big strong spoon, put 6 "gobs" equally on each sheet. Pat by hands evenly to edges, wetting hands with a little warm water if dough sticks to them.

Bake one sheet at a time (keep other in fridge) in a preheated 350° oven for 12-15 minutes until it's just browned. Let it cool slightly, cut in small squares, and ice while still in the pan. Remove each piece and place on paper to cool. Pack in tins with waxed paper or plastic wrap between layers and keep refrigerated.

# DESSERTS

**Lebkuchen Frosting:**
Add to 2 cups powdered sugar enough milk until you get a good spreading consistency. Add one tsp. each vanilla and almond extract. Divide frosting into two parts and apply to warm cookie bars with a pastry brush.

*"Spinning on high wheel"*        *Great Smoky Mt. National Park*

**\*Note:** You can find citron during the holidays at any grocery store or a natural foods store throughout the year. Or you can make your own out of candied citrus rinds as Grammie would have in the 1920's. Substituting dried pineapple and apricots for the citron works well, too.

## RUTH & GRACE'S RAISIN COOKIES

*Ruth and Grace Link were two elderly sisters who lived next door to us in West Va. when I was quite small. I remember munching these puffy cookies while swinging in the back yard.*

Plump 2 cups raisins in 1 cup boiling water.
Beat until fluffy:

| | |
|---|---|
| 1 cup butter | ½ tsp. nutmeg |
| 2 cups sugar | 1 tsp. cinnamon |
| 1 tsp. salt | ½ tsp. allspice |

Add and beat well:
- 3 eggs
- 1 tsp. baking powder
- 1 tsp. vanilla

Add the raisins and 4 cups flour until combined. Chill and drop by teaspoon onto a greased baking sheet. Bake at 350° for about 10 minutes.

# Desserts

Whenever my sisters and I would visit our grandmother's house as kids, we'd head straight for the cookie jars. She kept two large shelf-paper-covered shortening containers filled with her cookies. We knew we'd always find pumpkin cookies in one, sugar and chocolate cookies in the other. And they were puffy and soft. We didn't eat them in front of her...we'd sneak 'em. Somehow those containers stayed magically full. These are her recipes:

## Pumpkin Cookies

2 cups flour
2 cups sugar
2 tsp. cinnamon
¼ tsp. cloves
1 tsp. baking powder
1 cup raisins

½ tsp. salt
1 tsp. soda
1 cup soft butter
1 can pumpkin
1 egg

Cream butter and sugar, add egg, pumpkin, then dry ingredients, and raisins. Drop by spoonfuls onto greased cookie sheet. Bake at 375° for 10-15 minutes.

Grandfather's store                    Smith Brothers Grocery, Salem W. Va.

# DESSERTS

*Great-grandfather I.D. Smith and his Grocery*

## DROPPED SUGAR COOKIES

1 cup sugar
½ butter, softened
1 egg
½ cup buttermilk

1½ cup flour
½ tsp. soda
1 tsp. baking powder
1 tsp. vanilla

Beat sugar, butter, egg, and vanilla until fluffy. Add butter-milk and dry ingredients, and mix well. Drop by spoonfuls on a greased cookie sheet and sprinkle with coarse sugar or decorations. Bake about 12 minutes at 375° or until lightly browned.

## CHOCOLATE SUGAR COOKIES

Add 1½ squares unsweetened baker's chocolate to the butter mixture and ½ cup each walnuts and raisins after you stir in the dry ingredients. Bake the same as above.

### Kitchen Wisdom
•*A wise bee knows the sweetest honey is made from bitter flowers.*
•*A hungry rooster keeps quiet when he finds a worm.*
•*Don't measure my quart by your half-bushel.*[5]

# DESSERTS

## LEMON PIE CAKE

*If you bring this pie to a pot-luck party, people will say something like "What IS that?" It's a lemon pie with a little bit of cake on top that's sure to fascinate folks.*

1 cup sugar
¼ cup flour
3 Tbs. butter
1 pie shell, unbaked

2 eggs, separated
2 lemons, juice & rind
1 cup whole milk

Combine sugar, flour, butter, and egg yolks, beating until smooth. Beat in lemon juice and rind. Add milk slowly while stirring so it doesn't curdle. Beat egg whites until stiff and fold into lemon mixture. Bake the pie shell briefly (about 5 minutes), and pour in filling. Bake about 30-45 minutes at 350° until filling is firm.

> *Golden as a fall sunset, light as a fleecy sky,*
> *Lucious as a sun kissed-berry; that, my friends, is a pie!*[4]

## CHOCOLATE PUDDING CAKE

*Another fascinating bridge party dessert from the 1950's.*

1 cup flour
½ tsp. salt
1 tsp. baking powder
3 Tbs. butter
1 ²/₃ cup hot water

1 cup white sugar
¹/₃ cup cocoa powder
½ cup whole milk
1 tsp. vanilla

Combine flour, salt, baking powder and rub in butter. Add ½ sugar, 3 Tbs. cocoa, milk, vanilla and stir well. Pour into a greased 8 inch square baking dish. Sprinkle the top with the rest of the cocoa and sugar. Pour hot water over the top and bake at 350° for 30-40 minutes. Cake will be on the top, pudding on the bottom. Serve warm.

# DESSERTS

A unt Nell was my Grandmother Maudie's younger sister who lived in Alabama. I can still hear her heavy southern drawl as I read these words she wrote fifty years ago:

*Dearest Maudie;*
*In commemoration of a lovely visit, I hearby dedicate this cake recipe to you...in memory of the many pieces we consumed with our coffee!!!*

*Loving you always,*
*Nell*

## AUNT NELL'S POUND CAKE

1 cup solid veg. shortening
1¾ cup sugar
1 tsp. vanilla
Pinch salt

2 cups flour
5 eggs
5 Tbs. orange juice

Cream shortening and sugar. Add 2 Tbs. flour alternately with egg until all are used (beginning and ending with flour). Add orange juice and vanilla. Beat 150 strokes. Pour into a greased tube pan and bake for 1 hour at 300° until springy and lightly browned.

*"Dinner on the grounds"*                    *East Tennessee State University*

# DESSERTS

## LUELLA'S BLUEBERRY CAKE WITH LEMON BUTTER SAUCE

2 cups flour
2 tsp. baking powder
½ tsp. salt
1 egg

1 cup milk
1 cup sugar
1 Tbs. butter
2 cups fresh blueberries

Grease and flour a 9 inch square cake pan. Cream butter and sugar. Add beaten egg into first mixture. Combine dry ingredients and add to egg mixture alternately with milk. Coat berries with a small amount of flour, then add to mixture. Bake at 375° for about 30 minutes.

**Lemon Butter Sauce**:

¾ cup sugar
3 Tbs. cornstarch
2-4 Tbs. butter

1 cup water
2 lemons
1 tsp. vanilla

Melt butter and stir in sugar. Mix cornstarch in with ½ cup cold water until dissolved. Add remaining water and lemon juice and rind to melted butter mixture. Boil until clear. Take off heat and add vanilla. Pour over cake as you serve.

*This old-timey recipe originally called for one cup butter and vinegar instead of lemon juice. If you're watching your fat intake, the cake tastes good by itself.*

Great Smoky Mt. National Park

Mrs. Enloe, age 84, going fishing

### Face Superstitions

•*A dimple in your chin, many lovers you shall win.*
•*Itching left eye, a sign you will cry.*
•*If your lower lip itches, a short person will kiss you.*
•*If the eyebrows meet, you'll be a criminal..or rich..or both.*[9]

# Desserts

I *'ve tried and tried to make these Eastern European treats the way my mother-in-law, Lori Erbsen, does...but she has the special touch! While Lori learned much about life from her wise mother, she didn't learn to bake at home. "My mother was a food purist," says Lori of Molly Mandelblatt, who emigrated to America from Poland in 1910. Being very health conscious, Molly made her strudel without sugar...just a little honey on top. She owned a fruit market in Los Angeles and cooked only with fresh ingredients. Molly didn't trust commercially manufactured or canned foods; indeed, the worst of produce made it's way into cans in the late 19th and early 20th centuries. Lori says the only cans she ever saw her mother open were tomato sauce and pineapple. Unless you've eaten Lori's own strudel and rugelah, you'll be happy with the way these tasty morsels present themselves!*

*Molly Mandelblatt and daughter, Lori Erbsen*

## Lori's Apricot Strudel

2 cups flour
2 sticks butter or marg., softened
8 oz. sour cream

Mix these ingredients well and chill overnight. Divide into four sections, rolling out each portion into a rectangular shape about as thick as a pie crust.

Cover with:     **Apricot/Pineapple jam**
**Chopped walnuts**
**White raisins**
**Grated coconut**

Roll up jellyroll fashion and bake ½ hour at 350° on a greased cookie sheet. When cool, slice in diagonal slices about ½ inch thick.

# DESSERTS

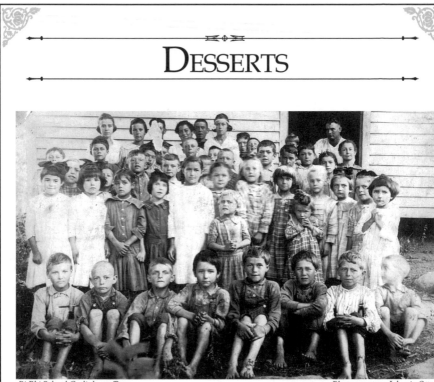

Pi Phi School Gatlinburg, Tenn.                    Photo courtesy Johnnie Otto

## LORI'S CINNAMON RUGELAH

*My husband, Wayne, and his sister, Bonnie, used to call these Uggabugga.*

| | |
|---|---|
| 2 sticks butter, softened | 3 cups flour |
| $^1/_3$ cup sugar | 1 egg yolk |
| 1 pkg. dried yeast | 8 oz. sour cream |

Stir yeast into sour cream. Cream butter and sugar and add egg yolk. Mix in sour cream and then add flour, combining well. Chill dough. Divide dough into 4 portions.

Combine:
1 cup sugar
1 cup finely chopped walnuts
2 tsp. cinnamon

Roll out each section of dough onto a piece of waxed paper (that's been sprinkled with some of the sugar/nut mixture) into a circle ¼ inch thick. Sprinkle top with more sugar mixture and cut into wedges. Roll up each wedge starting with large end and place on a greased cookie sheet. Bake at 350° for about 15 minutes until browned.

# DESSERTS

## Recipe Titles Hand-Written Into An 1885 Cookbook:

*Cure for Diptheria*
*Mrs. Mave's Nice Yeast Cake*
*Apple Jelly Pie*
*Cake Good*
*Aunt Alice's Custard Cake*
*Miss Bingham's Yeast Bread*

## CAKE GOOD, 1896

"2 eggs, 1 cup sugar, a little salt, 1 cup sweet cream, 2 teaspoonfuls baking powder in flour. Lemon or anything."

*Photo by Margaret Morley*                    *N.C. Dept. Archives and History*

## Kitchen Insults

- *Your brain rattles in a mustard-seed like buckshot in a coffee pot.*
- *You're grinnin' like a baked possum.*
- *Your eyes stick out like a peeled onion.*

# DESSERTS-ROMANCE

## PECAN WEDDING COOKIES

½ cup butter, softened
4 Tbs. sugar
1 tsp. vanilla
Powdered sugar

1 cup ground pecans
1 cup flour
Pinch salt

Combine butter, sugar, vanilla and beat until fluffy. Add flour and salt, and combine well. Stir in pecans. Roll into one inch balls and place on a greased cookie sheet spaced close together. Bake in a 300° oven about 20-25 minutes until just slightly browned. While still warm, roll in powdered sugar.

### You Won't Get Married If...
- *Someone sweeps under your feet.*
- *You take the last biscuit on the plate.*
- *You eat the point of your pie.*
- *You sit on the table.*
- *You fall up the steps.*

### Courtin'...1860's Style
- *I love you as sure as eggs is eggs.*
- *Your face is as smooth as eggshells.*
- *Your hands are as white as the belly of a flat fish.*[8]

*Grandfather Isadore Swell and his bride, Bessie*

### Advice to Lovers
- *Before marriage, keep both eyes open; after, shut one.*
- *Compliment another man's wife and endanger your life.*
- *A weddin' without courtin' is like vittles without salt.*

# ROMANCE

## WHO WILL YOU MARRY?

- If you sleep with a piece of wedding cake under your pillow, you'll dream of the one you'll marry.
- If the sun shines while it's raining, turn over a rock and if you find a hair, it will be the color of your future spouse's.
- On New Year's Eve, go from one room to another and throw a shoe over your shoulder. Now look in the mirror and you'll see the one you'll marry.
- Count fifty white horses, and the first unmarried man you shake hands with after counting the fiftieth will be the man you will marry.
- Recite this poem while looking over your shoulder at the new moon:

> *New moon, new moon, let me see*
> *Who my husband is to be;*
> *The color of his hair, the clothes he wears,*
> *And the happy day he is wed to me.*[5]

### Who Shouldn't You Marry?

- *Beware of that man,*
  *Be he friend or brother,*
  *Whose hair is one color,*
  *And his mustache another.*

- *When a briar attaches itself to the hem of a lady's apron, she should name it. If it sticks, her lover is dependable; if it drops, so should she drop him.*

- *If a girl wets her apron at washing, she will have a drunken husband.*[10]

# ROMANCE

## Choosing a Wedding Gown

*Marry in green, ashamed to be seen.*
*Marry in brown, a house in town.*
*Marry in red, wish you were dead.*
*Marry in yellow, ashamed of the fellow.*
*Marry in blue, you've chosen true.*
*Marry in white, and you marry all right.*[5]

## Love and Feet

*If your second toe is longer than the great toe, you will rule your mate.*[9]

## LOVE AND APPLES

- If you hold an apple in your armpit until it's warm and then eat it, your sweetheart will love you.
- A peel that's been removed from an apple without making a break can be thrown over the left shoulder to form the initial of the person that you will marry.
- Name apple seeds and shoot them at the ceiling. The one that hits the ceiling shows which one loves you best.
- Name 5 apple seeds and stick them to your forehead. The first to fall off tells who you will marry.
- Put an apple seed on each eyelid. Name each seed. The first to fall off will tell who you will marry.[9]

# ROMANCE

## KISS AND TELL

As lightly as your love for me,
I bore my love for you.
And knowing you would kiss and tell,
I kissed and tattled too.

Until continuous reports
And whispers unabated-
Revealed I only kissed and told,
But you exaggerated!

-Stella Weston Tuttle

## LOVE RHYMES

• Stump your toe, kiss your thumb, you'll see your beau 'fore bedtime comes.
• Happy's the wooin' not long a doin'.
• Marry when the year is new, your mate will be constant, kind, and true.
• If when you marry, your dress is red, you'll wish to God that you was dead; if when you marry your dress is white, everything will be all right.

### Sweet Dreams

*This Friday night I go to bed.*
*I place this night cap under my head.*
*To dream of the living and not of the dead,*
*To dream of the one that I should wed.*[5]

# FOLK REMEDIES

H ere are some interesting old-timey folk remedies and medical superstitions collected form Georgia, North Carolina, Kentucky, and Arkansas. Most of these "cures" are more dangerous than the malady they're intended to treat, so please, don't go drinking "pain ants" or putting sewing machine oil on your burns!

## TO CURE BACKACHE
• Let a seventh child walk seven times up and down your back.[9]
• Lie down and roll toward the first dove you hear cooing in the Spring, and your backache will be cured.[5]
• Boil pine tree roots and pain ants in clean cloth and place on the sore back.[5]
• Rub the sufferer's back against a tree where a hog has rubbed itself.[5]

## STYE
• Walk backwards to a cross-roads and spit on the ground three times over the right shoulder. The stye will leave you and infect the next passer-by. You can say "Stye, stye, leave my eye, and catch the first person that passes by."[9]
• Tell the person with the stye that he's told a lie, and it will go away.[9]

## EYE PROBLEMS
• Wear earrings to prevent blindness.[9]
• Bottled snow water is good for sore eyes.[9]
• Wash sore eyes in a mule trough.[5]
• For weak eyes, grow a mustache, clean glasses with hornets' nests or wear a green ring.

"Aunt Sophie smoking a handmade clay pipe, 1931."
Great Smoky Mt. National Park

# FOLK REMEDIES

## TO CURE CHICKEN-POX
• Sit in the henhouse for an hour.[9]

## SORE THROAT
• Take off your right sock at night and while it's warm, tie it around your neck. Let it remain there all night.

 **Old and Young** find a healing wonder for all inflammations of the Skin in

• Let a man who has smoked several years blow his breath down the sore throat.

# Comfort Powder

• Place a live toad against swollen tonsils and the swelling will disappear.
• If you drink water out of a stranger's shoe, your sore throat will be cured.[9]

## TO CURE TOOTH-ACHE
• Promise not to cut your nails or do similar things on Sunday.
• Pick up a rock, spit under it, and put it back like it was.[9]
• Have a tooth doctor write a word on a piece of paper, fold it many times, tie a string around it and hang it from his neck while saying some mysterious words.[5]

---

### Kitchen Wisdom

*The soul would have no rainbow had the eyes no tears.*
> -John Vance Cheney

*Praise loudly, blame softly.*
> -Catherine II

*Twixt optimist and pessimist,*
*The difference is droll;*
*The optimist sees the doughnut,*
*The pessimist, the hole.*

# FOLK REMEDIES

## HEADACHE
•Carry a nut in a pocket. Stroke it constantly.
•Wear a match in your hair to prevent headache.
•Long hair will cure headaches.[5]

## BLEEDING
•String nine buttons and tie them around your neck.
•"Spider webs are applied to the cut to staunch the flow of blood, for that is what house spiders were created for, and it is bad luck to destroy them or their webs."[5]

## TO STOP NOSEBLEED
•Drop a key down the back of the sufferer.[9]
•Drop sissors down your back.[5]
•Tie a red yarn string around your thumb.[9]
•Wear a certain gristle taken from a hog's ear.[9]

## TO CURE RHEUMATISM
•Steal an Irish potato and carry it in the pocket.[5]
•Make a salve of stolen butter.[5]

## BURNS
•Blow on the burn, repeating these words: "Three angels from the north; Go out fire, come in frost."[9]
•Apply a poultice of butter, the white of an egg, or soda and sewing machine oil.[5]

# FOLK REMEDIES

## To Cure Chills and Fever
•Pull down the cover as if going to bed, then get under the bed. The chills and fever will be fooled and leave you alone.
•Crawl down the stairs headfirst just before the time for the "rigor" to set in.[5]
•Hang onions in the house and if anyone in the room has a fever, it will go to the onions.[5]

## Typhoid and Smallpox
•Get smallpox (and you won't get typhoid).
•To prevent smallpox, carry an onion in your pocket.[9]
•Cut a chicken in half and put one part against the sole of each foot.

*"Washing clothes in Cades Cove, 1915" Great Smoky Mt. National Park*

### Kitchen Wisdom
•*Bad breath is better than no breath at all.*
•*A man who will never change his mind...
may not have any mind to change!*
•*Gossips drink and talk; frogs drink and squawk.*

# WEATHER LORE

## SIGNS OF A COLD WINTER
•The number of snows in December subtracted from 31 will give you the total number of snows that winter. (A snow is counted as a snowfall if you can track a goose on a board.)
•Thickening of the feathers of a rooster's legs
•Thickening of the fur on a possum's back
•Cornshucks are thick
•Bark on trees is thick
•Heavy berry crop in summer

## SIGNS OF BAD WEATHER
•The cat lies with its back to the fire
•A great many women stirring around
•Roosters crow on one foot
•Pigs squeal
•Evening red, morning gray, sets the traveller on his way.
•Evening gray, morning red, sets the traveller in his bed.

*Photo courtesy of Richard Renfro*

## SIGNS OF FAIR WEATHER
•No weather is ill if the wind be still.
•A bright clear-faced moon
•Ants running around
•If all the bread is eaten at the table,
  The next day will be clear.

## SIGNS THE WEATHER'S CHANGING
•When frogs croak...Winter's broke.
•Spring is near when the robins appear.
•Winter is near when the blackbirds appear.
•If February first is fair and clear,
  The Winter's half done for the year.

# WEATHER LORE

## SIGNS OF RAIN

Stepping on ants
Flies bite
Smoke goes to the ground
Your head itches
Broken bones ache
A horse with an unusually fluffy mane[5]

You kill a spider
A peacock screams
Frogs croak
Your nose itches
Corns on feet hurt

### Rain Rhymes

- *When clouds appear like rocks and flowers,*
  *The earth's refreshed with frequent showers.*
- *When the stars begin to huddle,*
  *The Earth will soon be in a puddle.*
- *When the peacock loudly bawls,*
  *Soon we'll have both rain and squalls.*
- *A morning rain is like an old maid's dancing...*
  *It soon gives out!*

## WHEN TO FISH

When the wind is in the East,
Then the fishes bite the least;
When the wind is in the West,
Then the fishes bite the best;
When the wind is in the North,
Then the fishes do come forth;
When the wind is in the south,
It blows the bait in the fish's mouth.

## HOW TO GET A GOOD CROP

- If seeds are placed in water where lightning-struck wood is soaked, the crop will be bountiful.
- You will have a good crop if you carry a horse-chestnut.
- Sow your turnips the 25th of July, you'll make a good crop, wet or dry.
- Plant your corn when the leaves of the oak tree are as big as squirrel ears.

# Hearth Crafts

**W**hat women once called chores of necessity have now become merely hobbies. We don't need candles to see at night and don't need to make them even if we want them, but it's still fun....especially if we're not making enough for the whole winter! Here are a couple of crafts from things you can find at the grocery store, or that you can grow yourself. If you have sun and a corner of your yard you're tired of mowing, plant a package of birdhouse gourd seeds. There are a million things you can make with them from birdhouses to spoons to dolls to Gourdaments!

## Gourdaments

You'll need:
- Small, dried birdhouse gourds
- Dried flowers
- Hot glue gun
- Twine

Directions:

Cut a hole in the front middle of the gourd (to look like a small birdhouse). Tie the dried flowers into a bundle and glue them to the inside of the gourd with the flowers sticking out of the whole. Poke two holes in the top of the gourd to thread some twine through for hanging. Hang them on a hearth or tree...they'll keep for years.

---

### Cheese and Butter Insults

- *She's so mean, butter wouldn't melt in her mouth (if we had any to put in there). 1833*
- *He's as contrary as cheese that won't set. 1845*
- *She don't know cheese from chalk! 1844*[8]

---

# Hearth Crafts

## Squash Lanterns

**You'll need:**
- A small butternut squash
- Twine
- A metal-bottomed tea candle

**Directions:**
Cut a round hole in the back of the squash and scoop out the seeds. Carve a Halloween face or design on the opposite side of the squash with a pocket knife. Poke a piece of a bamboo skewer through the top of the squash. Tie twine to the skewer to hang. Secure the candle inside. Hang your lighted lantern in a window or from your chandelier. (Keep an eye on it while it's lit.)

*Photo courtesy of Great Smoky Mt. National Park*

## Kitchen Wisdom

- *A new broom sweeps clean, but an old brush knows the corners.*
- *The finer the curd, the better the cheese.*

# Chores

## When to Wash

Wash on Monday, you'll have all week to dry.
Wash on Tuesday, not so much awry.
Wash on Wednesday, not so much to blame.
Wash on Thursday, wash for shame.
Wash on Friday, wash for need.
Wash on Saturday, you're a big goose indeed.

Photo by Margaret Morely N.C. Dept. Archives & History

## The Laundry, 1885

• Do not have beefsteak for dinner on washing or ironing days. Don't have fried or broiled fish. The smell sticks and the clothes will not be sweet.
• As for vegetables, do not have spinach, peas, stringbeans, or applesauce. They take too long to prepare. Have potatoes, macaroni, sweet corn, or stewed tomatoes instead.[6]

## "Out of the frying-pan

into the fire." Take care that you don't go that way, when you try to make your washing easier. Better be sure of what you're doing. Get **Pearline**, the original washing-compound, the best-known, the fully-proved.

There are plenty of imitations of it. But even if they're not dangerous—and some are—they're not economical.

**Pearline** used properly, goes farther, does more work, and saves more wear, than anything else that's safe to use.

## Millions ^NOW_USE Pearline

# CHORES

B ack in the days when the only way to get butter was to churn it, folks found they had to count on superstition in order to get the butter to "make." Sometimes it would, sometimes not. In centuries past, witches were believed to be the cause of most butter-making failures. Abundant folklore can be found to help churners ward off the bad butter witches. Here are but a few possibilities:

## TO DRIVE BUTTER WITCHES AWAY:

- Boil sweet milk on the fire and stir it with a fork.
- Place a dime under the hearth.
- Crush egg shells after the egg has been removed so the witches won't use them for boats.
- Burn salt in the fireplace to drive away witches or to keep them from coming down the fireplace.
- If you hang a bread sifter on a doorknob at night, you will find trapped witches in it in the morning.

N.C. Dept. Archives and History

### For Successful Butter-Making...

*Get the ugliest person you know to look into the cream jar and it will turn so you can churn it.*

# HEIRLOOM SEEDS

**Burpee's Seeds**
Heirloom Seed Catalog
300 Park Ave.
Warminster, PA 18974-0008

**The Cook's Garden**
PO Box 65
Londonderry, VT 05148

**J.L. Hudson, Seedsman**
PO Box 1058
Redwood City, CA 94064
Catalog $1.00

**J.W. Jung Seed Co.**
335 S. High St.
Randolph, WI 53957

**Shepherd's Garden Seeds**
30 Irene St.
Torrington, CT 06790

**Johnny's Selected Seeds**
299 Foss Hill Rd.
Albion, ME 14910

**Pinetree Garden Seeds**
Box 300
New Glouster, ME 04260

**Seeds of Change**
PO Box 15700
Santa Fe, NM 87506-5700

**R.H. Shumway**
PO Box 1
Graniteville, SC 29829

**Southern Exposure
Seed Exchange**
PO Box 170
Earlysville, VA 22936

# CREDITS

## BOOKS

1. Boatright, Hudson, and Maxwell, *Texas Folk and Folklore,* So. Methodist University Press, Dallas, TX, 1954.
2. Brown, Frank C., *North Carolina Folklore*, UNC Press Chapel Hill, NC, 1964.
3. de Lys, Claudia, *A Treasury of American Superstitions,* Philosophical Library, New York, NY.
4. Harrison County Extension Homemakers, *WVA Heritage Cookbook,* 1976.
5. Killion, Ronald and Waller, Charles, *A Treasury of Georgia Folklore*, Cherokee Publishing Company, Atlanta, GA, 1972.
6. *Practical Housekeeping*, Buckeye Publishing Co., Minneapolis, MN, 1885.
7. Randolph, Vance, *Ozark Superstitions*, Dover Publishing, Inc., New York, N.Y., 1946.
8. Taylor, Archer & Whiting, Bartlett, *American Proverbs and Proverbial Phrases 1820-1880*, Belknap Press of Harvard University Press, Cambridge, MA, 1958.
9. Thomas, Daniel and Thomas, Lucy, *Kentucky Superstitions*, Princeton University Press, Princeton, NJ, 1920.
10. Wilson, Charles, *Backwoods America*, UNC Press, Chapel Hill, NC, 1934.

## PHOTOGRAPHIC CREDITS

Blue Ridge Parkway, US Dept. Interior, Nat. Park Service
East Tennessee State University Photographic Archives
Great Smoky Mt. National Park Photographic Archives
Mars Hill College, So. Appalachian Photographic Archives
N.C. Dept. of Archives and History
Johnnie Otto, family photos
Lila Swell, Leon Swell, Nancy Smith Swell, family photos
Wayne Erbsen, back cover photo

# CREDITS

## THANKS!

To my grandmother, Maude Smith…whose wisdom and kindness I remember whenever I set to cooking. To my husband, Wayne Erbsen, for support and tireless taste testing. To recipe/story contributors: Nancy & Leon Swell, Lori Erbsen, Pam Budd, Jean Harrison & Chris Rogers, Johnnie Otto, Marti Otto, Richard Renfro, Martha Whaley, Laura Swell Wright, Janet Swell, Bonnie Erbsen Neustein, and Steve Webb. To Steve Millard for cover art and graphic design, Janet Swell, Nancy Swell, and Lori Erbsen for editing, and Tracy McMahon for content ideas. Food testers included: Annie, Wes & Rita Erbsen, Justin Hallman, Tracy McMahon, Pam Budd, Lucas & Kyle Rogers, and just about everybody who walked in our door this year.

## Kitchen Wisdom

- *Be what you is and not what you ain't, cause if you ain't what you is, you is what you ain't.*
- *It is better to be a has-been than a never-was.*
- *You can't make the cookies when you haven't got the dough.*

# MY FAMILY RECIPES

# MY FAMILY RECIPES

# My Family Recipes

# MY FAMILY RECIPES

# MY FAMILY RECIPES

# My Family Recipes

# BOOKS & RECORDINGS
## *On*
# Native Ground Music

## INSTRUCTION BOOKS

Bluegrass Banjo for the
   Complete Ignoramus!
Clawhammer Banjo for the
   Complete Ignoramus!
Painless Mandolin Melodies
Southern Mountain Banjo
Southern Mountain Dulcimer
Southern Mountain Fiddle
Southern Mountain Guitar
   Southern Mountain Mandolin
   Starting Bluegrass Banjo
      From Scratch

## BOOKS OF SONGS & LORE

Backpocket Bluegrass Songbook
Backpocket Old-Time Songbook
Ballads & Songs of the Civil War
Cowboy Songs, Jokes, Lingo 'n Lore
Crawdads, Doodlebugs &
   Creasy Greens
Log Cabin Cooking
Old-Time Gospel Songbook
Outlaw Ballads, Legends & Lore
Railroad Fever
Rural Roots of Bluegrass
Take Two & Butter 'Em While They're Hot
The Lost Art of Pie Making

## RECORDINGS

Authentic Outlaw Ballads
Ballads & Songs of the
   Civil War
Bullfrogs On Your Mind
Cold Frosty Morning
Cowboy Songs of the
   Wild Frontier
Crawdads, Doodlebugs &
   Creasy Greens
Old-Time Gospel Favorites

Old-Time Gospel Instrumentals
Pierre Cruzatte
   - Lewis & Clark
Raccoon and a Possum
Rural Roots of Bluegrass
Songs of the Santa Fe Trail
Southern Mountain Classics
Southern Soldier Boy
The Home Front
Waterdance

*Other Great Books by BARBARA SWELL:*

**Children at the Hearth
Log Cabin Cooking
Mama's in the Kitchen
Old-Time Farmhouse Cooking
Secrets of the Great Old-Timey Cooks
The Lost Art of Pie Making**

Write or call for FREE Catalog
NATIVE GROUND MUSIC
109 Bell Road, Asheville, NC 28805
Call: 828-299-7031 or 800-752-2656
FAX: 828-298-5607

Email
banjo@nativeground.com
WEB SITE
www.nativeground.com

# RECIPE INDEX